Nature ~ IQ

"Let's Survive, Not Die!"

~Keith Alan Hamilton~

inner child press, ltd.

CREDITS

Author

~Keith Alan Hamilton~

Prose Editing

Madeline Sharples

Photography

Jenna Lindberg

~Keith Alan Hamilton~

Cover(s) Photography

Jenna Lindberg

GENERAL INFORMATION

Nature ~ IQ

~Keith Alan Hamilton~

1st Edition : 2013

This Publishing is protected under Copyright Law as a "Collection". All rights for all submissions are retained by the Individual Author and or Artist. No part of this Publishing may be Reproduced, Transferred in any manner without the prior **WRITTEN CONSENT** of the "Material Owner" or its Representative Inner Child Press. Any such violation infringes upon the Creative and Intellectual Property of the Owner pursuant to International and Federal Copyright Law. Any queries pertaining to this "Collection" should be addressed to Publisher of Record.

Publisher Information

1st Edition : Inner Child Press :
intouch@innerchildpress.com
www.innerchildpress.com

This Collection is protected under U.S. and International Copyright Laws

Copyright © 2013 : ~Keith Alan Hamilton~

LOC # : 1-1057439001

ISBN-13 : 978-0615935577 (Inner Child Press, Ltd.)
ISBN-10 : 0615935575

$ 24.95

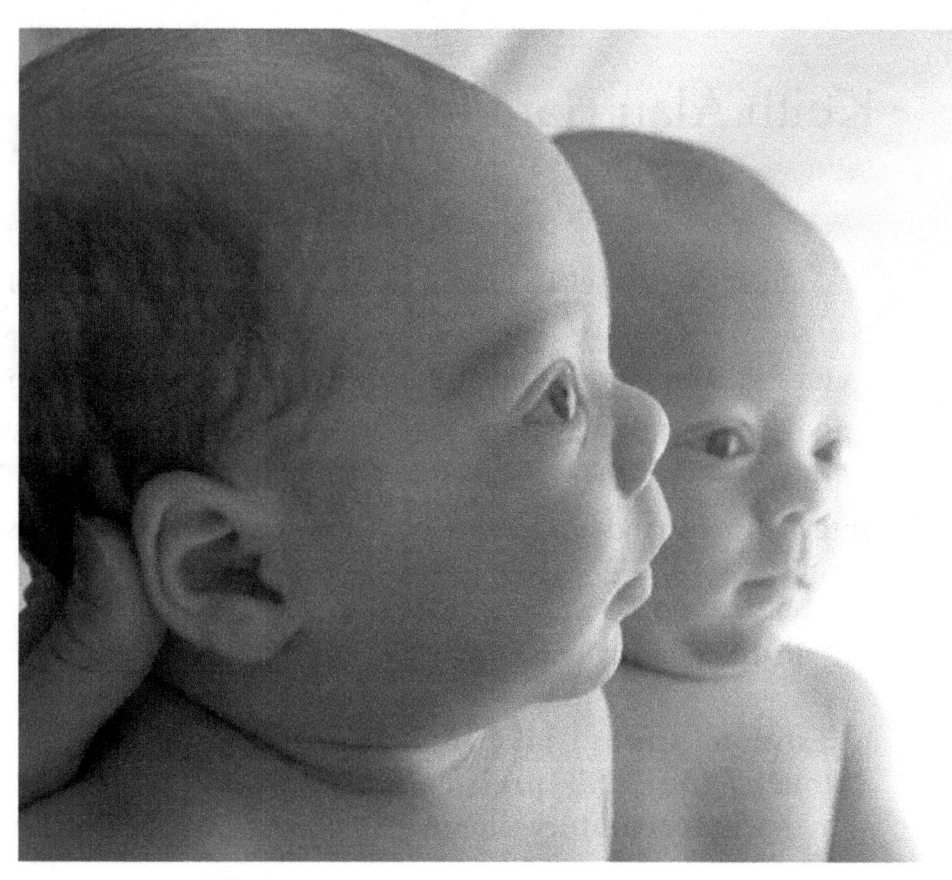

Photography by Jenna Lindberg

Dedication

To my children,

my children's children

their children, and their children's children,

and the future survival of the humankind.

Photography by Jenna Lindberg

Foreword

It's rare that someone can pick up an author's work and say "I know the man!" It is far less likely that you know the author's roots, his family and friends, his hurts and his triumphs… I am proud to say that I really do! This gives me a wonderful insight, a "front row" seat to view what Keith Hamilton is sharing with us. Don't feel cheated because there are only "great seats" to view what Keith is sharing with us in the following pages!

Our world is changing rapidly. We have immense economic, political and environment challenges NOW and in the immediate future. If we are to survive and indeed THRIVE… we all must make necessary adaptations starting today. Besides today's health and happiness, leaving a lasting, inspired and responsible legacy for our kids and grandkids are Keith's passion in all that he writes about!

Pretty heavy stuff? Yes! But don't worry about getting judged harshly or being pounded by ideology… my childhood friend simply introduces the vital issues in a personal and intimate way of sharing his own thoughts. What better way than sharing his heart and soul and love for his friends, family and country? Through great prose and wonderful illustration, Keith touches emotional nerves to get us to use our hearts and our minds. Let's not only survive these fast-changing times.. but be joyous and content!

What I know that you'll love most ….. is that you won't get answers, direction or a blueprint. Instead, you will see the world as it is and start thinking about what you CAN and MUST do to provide your own family and community a better life today. Picture your own loved ones on these pages and feel Keith Hamilton's passion for yourself.

Bruce Hahn
Houston, Texas

Photography by Jenna Lindberg

Preface

One of the methods back in 2012 other than print I chose to publish this book of poems, sayings, and more was online without charge over the internet, using a flip-book technology. My goal was to have as many people as possible take advantage of the freely accessible way I've communicated my thoughts. I offer those who choose to read my words the opportunity to hear my call to action regarding the survival of humankind.

I also waited until the last part of 2012 to promote the distribution of Nature ~ IQ: "Let's Survive, Not Die" in PDF format (free download) to demonstrate a positive voice that focuses on the most vital needs and issues of the people. 2012 was a year filled with the hype of doomsday prophesy and the campaign for election of the president of the United States. It was another election where our choices between candidates were once again devoid of timely concepts and practices that would help the people with immediate and long-term circumstances. Unlike those candidates for president, I've suggested a more cooperative, forward thinking, transitional and adaptive approach to established and new concepts and practices to be used not only by those who represent the people in government, but by *We the people* as well. Concepts and practices if more fully implemented will improve the people's lot in life and will create an environment that will make the people more self-reliant, more resilient, and less susceptible to disruptive conditions. In other words, we will create a support system that will help the people help themselves, no matter the issue or earth changes we may have to face.

As a concerned citizen, being a part of *We the people*, I've expressed in the best manner humanly possible, a nonpartisan voice echoing common sense and reason while doing so in the midst of all the 2012 commotion. It is a voice, if combined with the many, may over time possess greater value for all humanity.

In addition to my sayings and prose, I have chosen to use poetry, with its inherent capability to bring forth and express, to make more palatable the full flavor of any intelligently perceptive insight embedded in its words. Within the beat of poetry, the people can enjoy the insight and then hunger after the thoughts that make up the integral fabric of its character. The experience of such a creative process may inspire the people themselves to add more tasty ingredients or seasonings to the overall mix. Hopefully this process will help to create a recipe more palatable to all humanity. Although, some may suggest I've reduced the recipe for poetry into more of a prose-like mix. I feel my everyday free verse style, with its empathic twists and turns of perception, will be more satisfying to the taste buds of a broader spectrum of people. Words such as these may cause the use of a more multi–dimensional perspective when thinking about what is presented within this book, rather than the more traditional approach to poetry. We'll see.

This book is the introduction, the first in a series of books covering various topics highlighted in the prose, sayings and poems that follow. Don't hesitate to share it with as many people as you can – especially, if you feel it embodies a message spirited with hope and direction needing to be heard by *We the people*. More importantly, distribute it widely for the sake of our children,

~Keith Alan Hamilton~

~ * ~

"A society not concerned for the welfare of *the people*, neglecting to develop and maintain a system that's freely accessible and affordable in the areas of energy, information/education, transportation, housing and health care, is a society not intelligently progressive enough to envision the benefit to all in doing so; therefore, such a lack of insight, not learning from the acts of societies in the past, they make the ill-informed choice, which progresses the slow suicide and the overall demise of *the people*; how will *we the people* in our time choose?"

~ * ~

Table of Contents

Forward	vii
Preface	ix

Introduction   1

     beyond 2012   3

Featured Poems, Sayings and more…….. 13

Let's Survive, Not Die	14
if tomorrow comes	33
to freely live	37
Mother Earth: living our human way	41
my fellow humans	47
someway ~ somehow	51
humankind acts in a way	53
a new ~ Independence Day	63
if we say ~ peace	67
begin to heal ourselves	72
surviving earth change	76

Table of Contents... *continued*

Conclusion — 86
    a clear cut message — 90
    A few more sayings………. — 99

Postface — 111
    About the Author — 115
    The Photographer . . . Jenna Lindberg — 116
    Endorsements — 118
    ~Keith Alan Hamilton~ Links — 123

Nature ~ IQ

"Let's Survive, Not Die!"

~Keith Alan Hamilton~

~Keith Alan Hamilton~

Introduction

Hopefully, the thoughts in this book will motivate *We the people* to formulate a clear message that presents an united appeal with purpose – a resonating call enlisting the cooperation of those that represent *We the people* within government where a forthright, proactive, and concerned people justifiably ask for the assistance of the servant they appointed. Asking for the formation of a balanced partnership is centered on the theme of survival, the ongoing preservation of the human species. Such a balanced partnership is now more important than ever with drastically disruptive earth changes advancing steadily on the horizon.

If such a process of communication can be achieved between the government and *We the people*, it will serve as a model for other people in other nations as a relevant and timely choice to follow. To assure its purpose, keep its focus, and guarantee its ongoing success, we must maintain a nonpartisan way of thinking. It would have to be free from the distraction of assigning blame, name-calling, vendetta, and the over promotion of a certain cultural/national agenda. Its primary goal would be to come up with a more effective support system to help *We the people* to be more able to help ourselves.

Also, if this support system were to be effective, it would have to be focused around proven concepts and practices that are freely accessible and affordable to *We the people*. Whether the concepts and practices are old or new, they must have a forward thinking outlook in their development. Not so unlike the concepts and practices put forth by Alexander Hamilton to support the growth of a new nation, those used today and in the days that follow need to create employment, satisfy supply and demand, stabilize the economy, and inhibit chaotic conditions from materializing within *We the people*. These concepts and practices would have to be behaviorally, intelligently progressive by factoring in the relevant lessons of lived experience, our expanding Nature ~ IQ. They need to maintain a degree of flexibility and be transitional in their developmental process. This would help these concepts and practices remain adaptable to the conditions of the times, while using innovative technology. As such they would be fully able to adjust to the needs of *We the people* in the future.

The five key concepts and practices I focus on in this book, which to be effective, should be made freely accessible and affordable to *We the people* are: energy, information/education, transportation, health care, and housing. If we implement support systems focused around proven concepts and practices, which improve the overall condition of *We the people*, such a positive act will lift up the spirit of *We the people*. *We the people* will be more ready and able, more resilient and adaptive, and more willing and confident to creatively find ways to help ourselves and to survive any type of earth change that may occur in the years to come. No matter if these earth changes manifest themselves separately or in combination and regardless if these earth changes appear in forms, such as: climate change with more violent weather or through global plagues, super-volcanoes, killer asteroids, in an increased amount and intensity of earthquakes and tsunamis, human born nuclear war or terrorism, or maybe even the arrival of unfriendly extraterrestrials, etc.

If *We the people* are provided the proper supportive environment, afforded enough time and opportunity to find a way; then *We the people*, helping ourselves can and will be able to survive and adapt to whatever obstacle of change Nature and its earth throws upon us.

beyond 2012
gonna be more proactive

~ here's what
I'll be doing

not waiting around
or being held back
by some wacko prophesy
Nostradamus
Mayan calendar
global warming
earth change
~ bullshit ~
nope…..
all that ~ ain't gonna
decide my destiny
~ I'm
gonna be trying
given it my best
my all
to live
with a purpose
having a vision
that fills me with conviction
not only inspiring hope
within myself
but inside
all the people
I meet
along the streets
and byways
of my community
and the world
~ especially upon

Nature ~ I Q : Let's Survive, Not Die !

the electronic waves
that internet
just yammering
with free speech possibilities
and potential
so the people too ~
throughout the earth
can get a diverse perspective
on planetary events
 ~ then be more able to form
an informed opinion
from the basis of sound
judgment….. and then
will want to live on
to survive ~
prepare a way ~
construct a plan
for the future
of our children
and our children's ~ children
….. that's what I'm gonna
be doing ~ how 'bout you
my brothers
and sisters ~
~ the hell
with Nostradamus
that Mayan calendar
global warming
earth change…….
~ whatever
let's not buy into
the hopelessness
the helplessness
or paralysis
waiting to
weigh down ~

immobilize
the survival spirit
of humanity
within such a bleak reality
~ *We the people*
need to creatively
sculpture
our own reality
~   stand erect
and united
become
collectively
strong ~
impenetrable
and unstoppable as one
for one worthy purpose
and vision
above all else ~
the survival of humanity
~ *We the people*
of the planet
need to focus on
what's really happening
upon Nature's earth
not get lost in the mirage
of prediction and prophecy
we must go beyond
the right of free speech
and marching in the street
we need to let our
elected representative
the inspiring politician know
if you want to be voted in
be offering up ideas
strategies ~ plans
ways to help the people

Nature ~ I Q : Let's Survive, Not Die !

improve the condition
of the people
based on proven
and transitional
concepts and practices
within industries like ~
information/education ~
transportation ~
healthcare ~ housing
and energy
even beyond that…..
make
these
concepts and practices
freely accessible
and affordable for everyone
~ fully support
an infrastructure
that creates employment ~
satisfies supply and demand
and stabilizes the economy
~ or don't be asking
for our vote
 ~ 'cause you ain't hearing
the voice of the people
you're just offering up
some well-marketed
blather to get
yourself elected
~ listen up
we ain't asking for
no handout
some welfare
or communist state
just an improved system
as to the implementation

~Keith Alan Hamilton~

of these things mentioned ~
which will provide us
the people
with a willingness
an uplifted spirit
that will inspire in us
a drive that shall
produce our own
opportunities
the potential to.....
help ourselves ~
an industriousness ~
to develop the abilities
and hopefully
through our united efforts
we will allot ourselves
the precious time
to come up with ways
that will transition us past
and beyond
all the doom and gloom
2012 ~ Nostradamus
Mayan calendar
global warming
earth change
bullshit ~
'cause ~ *We the people*
ain't gonna be falling into
the lure of hopelessness
the vat of helplessness
or the straightjacket
of paralysis
but rather ~ beyond 2012
~ *We the people*
together
are gonna be

Nature ~ I Q : Let's Survive, Not Die !

more proactive
more prepared
more adaptive
instead of being
some reactionary
finger pointing
blamer
excuse maker
overburdened with guilt
from the mistakes
of simply being human
….. and no doubt
time and time again
Nature ~ it's earth
even ourselves….
will create day to day ills ~
as well as global tribulations
where ~ *We the people*
will just have to face
such changes
head on
and deal with them….

why….. what for ~
for who ~ you may ask ~
as said before…. to better assure
the survival of our kind
our children and our children's
children into the future

~ you've heard it right
my brothers and sisters

~ peace out

~Keith Alan Hamilton~

~ * ~

We the people of the United States, let's free ourselves from the misperceptions, the blame, the guilt and the inhibitions that surround earth change. Let's set the example, set the course, provide the guidance and then lead the rest of *We the people* on the earth to a bright and lasting future for all humanity.

~ * ~

Nature ~ I Q : Let's Survive, Not Die !

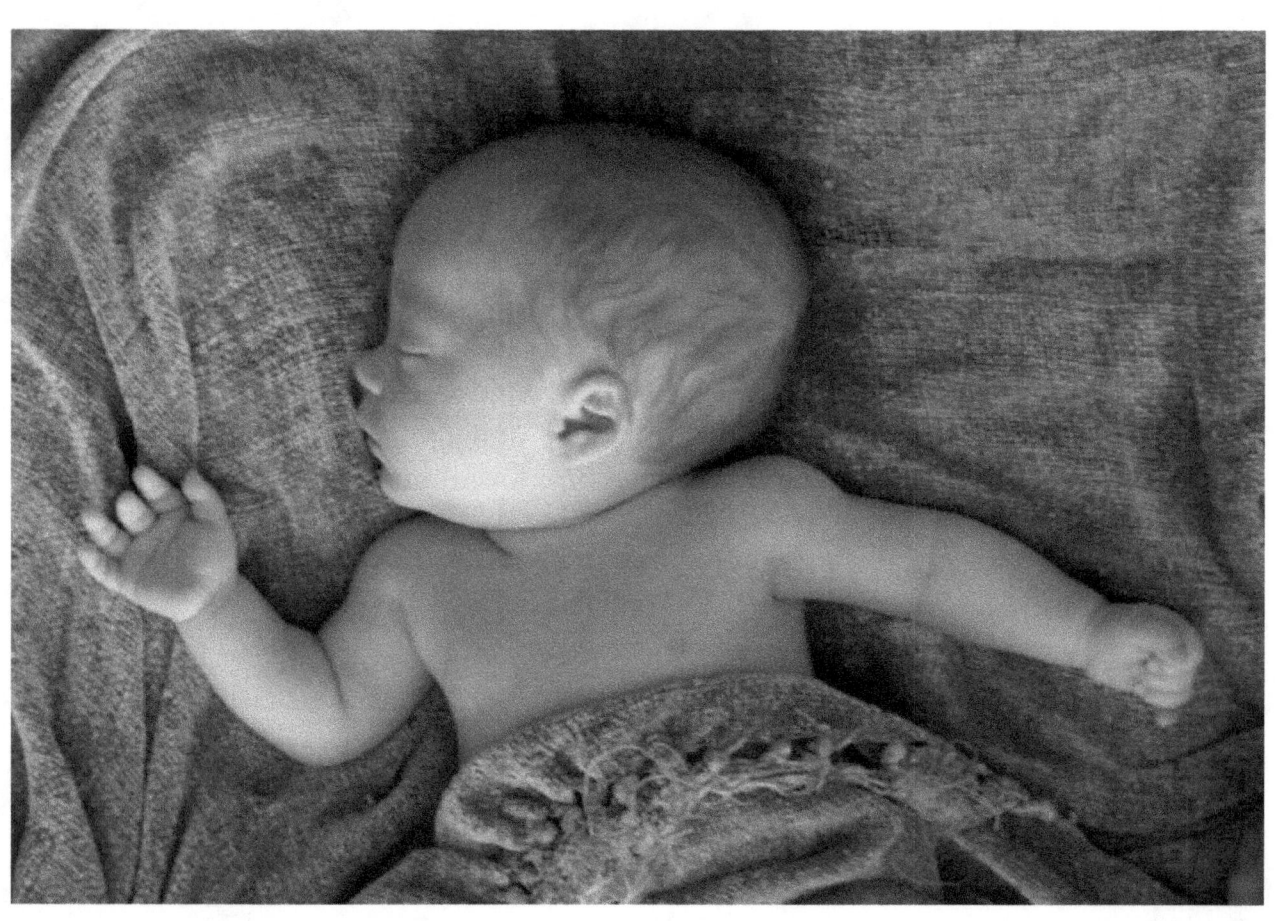

Photography by Jenna Lindberg

~Keith Alan Hamilton~

Photography by Jenna Lindberg

Nature ~ I Q : Let's Survive, Not Die !

~ * ~

"With earth changes ominously on the horizon, the cry of the protester for change to 'The People' and 'The Man' should be no longer, '*Make Love, Not War*,' but more urgently, Let's Survive, Not Die."

~ * ~

~Keith Alan Hamilton~

Featured

Poems,

Sayings

and

more………

~ Let's Survive, Not Die
the breadth of perception

        that cause of yesteryear
        you know ~ "the cause"
        what was stood for,
        marched for
        and sung for
        by the folk musician
        not so many,
        decades ago
        with its
        revolutionary
        consciousness
        which included
        the slogan
        "*Make Love, Not War*"
        and yet,
        seemingly
        its noble message
        has diminished
        somewhat over ~ time
        as to precedence
        wherefore,
        taking on a role of
        lesser import than before
        why you say ~
        'cause the focus
        for ~ the cause
        and the conditions
        giving it worth
        have started to shift
        due to circumstance
        from changing
        the ways of

~Keith Alan Hamilton~

human deficiency
full of plunder and waste
to being overshadowed
as the moon
during a solar eclipse
in that ~
~   the cause
way back then
is now becoming
out ~   staged
within the collective mind
of the people
because of the magnitude
given in the forecast
about earth change
tumultuously
and relentlessly
approaching
~   as if an ominous
storm on the horizon
of which is
plummeting
the purpose
of human aspiration
into a pattern
quite simply
focused around
that of mere survival
~ ~
yes ~
once again
like in the past
~ ~
well
I say,
under the shadow

Nature ~ I Q : Let's Survive, Not Die !

of all this doomsday
earth fever,
water rising,
draught spreading
extreme weather
forecasting
~ to hell then
with that so-called
mother earth analogy
to instill the prodigal child
with a guilt to bring forth
that act of repentance
and the eventual
returning to the flock
~ as if the imagery
contains real merit
for the ever emergent
state of affairs
'cause when you think
about it ~
earth
~ you ain't
really my mother
and will never,
ever ~ measure up
to my mom's
kind of love
where bringing
harm to me or others
was not in her thoughts
and as if
you could
really have thoughts
~ anyhow,
where you could then
somehow realize

~Keith Alan Hamilton~

what you are going to do
and then ~
through the grace
of your creator
be able to
reflect upon ~
reevaluate
what you will do
to those
supposedly
your children
~ ~
you ain't
my mother ~   earth
no more
than an earthquake
is my sister,
an erupting volcano
is my brother
or some whirling tornado
is my cousin
spinning a tall tale
that's fond to my ears
neither ~   either
could some
flooding river
from a torrential downpour
driven on by the gale force
of a powerful hurricane
pushing ashore,
were to somehow
possibly become
in my mind ~
like that moment of climax
blissfully uniting
me and my lover as ~ one

Nature ~ I Q : Let's Survive, Not Die !

to be jubilantly remembered
forevermore
~ ~
yeah right,
earth
I don't see how
that all gives me
some warm and cozy
nurturing,
motherly
kind of feeling
about you   ~
let's get real
~   come on now
people
the earth
and it's changing
systemic condition
can't think or worry
or even perceive
a concern for you or me
based on some
set of values,
what is right or wrong
to even begin to pronounce
and then impose
a fair and viable judgment
according to human
acts or deeds
~   the emotionless earth
will act now
and into the future
much like it
has in the past
by changing
its environment

to the point of no return
way, way beyond
the human ability
to fix or alter its course
and therefore
the earth
through
climate change
will kill ~ yep kill
similar to what it did
250 million years ago
when ~
95 percent of all life
during the Permian period
fuckin' perished
and what then
kept living,
was only due to
the luck of the draw
therein ~
much life was annihilated
caused by several factors
not just from one
action or thing
a combined process
void of reason
and the thought
of consequence
associated with
reflective consciousness
changed the recurrent
systemic ~
regulatory pattern
without hesitation
or remorse
on the earth's part

Nature ~ I Q : Let's Survive, Not Die !

~ ~
a system, which
humanity
hardly knows
a thing about
or even enough about
to claim ~   we
have the knowledge
to say,
we know how
that system
all works
even to begin to
possibly blame
the humankind
for any earth changes
that may happen
~ ~
therefore
and therein
the time wasted
through such misperception
getting us overly involved
in mitigation ~ intervention
instead of *proactive adaptation*
will only divert our attention
down the wrong road
leading us to the valley of death
~   those earth changes
that science is starting
to discover and then reveal
if all this is so,
~   you and me
our children
and their children
we'll need every moment

that can be gotten
or is left
to workout
some way ~ layout a plan
to save humanity
within the time allotted
as those like James Lovelock
have tried to predict
~ how can we pretend
or say,
we have the know how
to responsibly save
something else
as if we could prevent
those earth changes
surely to come
reverse or fix
a regulatory system's
breakdown
through the practice
of sustainable living
with an emphasis
on reducing
carbon emissions
by us humans
~ ~
if ~ yes if
we can't really,
even save
or change ourselves
especially our destructive
patterns of behavior
that the green movement
has been
asking us to amend
for years now

Nature ~ I Q : Let's Survive, Not Die !

while motivated
from the mantra
"save the earth"
~ ~
firstly
we,
the humankind
have to believe
we can
and will
prevail over
what will happen on earth
~   dispense away the guilt
the faultfinding
and move forward
with the goal to overcome
doing so   ~   from
much effort
within our thinking
paying attention and observing
what are the appropriate
type of things
for our
present time
and circumstance
while thinking upon
the things learned
from the experience
of how to live through
as revealed,
discovered
and remembered
about earth's forceful ways
improving our so-called
Nature ~ IQ,
progressing intelligently

until we know enough
to lift ourselves
as if above the earth
and beyond its rules
freeing ourselves
of the restrictions
entrapping us
through our beliefs of old
which has prolonged this
co-dependent relationship
as if a necessity
with the earth
that appears to be
barred of deviation
according to what
we've
thought
or only have known
fooling us to just live
without question
upon the earth
as the only way
things appear
~   making it seem
this one option
is
so ~ so
ingrained into us
as if to be
the one choice
or single means
for our survival
~   such a notion
seems deeply shrouded
within this inherent
aforementioned

Nature ~ I Q : Let's Survive, Not Die !

predisposition
where living on earth
and living by
its systemic way
is some benevolent
act of friendship
of motherhood
on the earth's part
while   ~   all along
holding us
as its dupe
within an oxygenated
bubble   ~   dome
death chamber
that's now undergoing
structural instability
within its recurrent pattern
of systemic order
that is somehow
the fault of its captives
even though,
the earth's system
~   for maintenance
~   for sustainability
were not freely revealed
to us slaves beforehand
giving us at least a choice
that could be clearly followed
~ ~
when   ~   when
will we awaken
from the cradle of our stupor
to clearly understand
in spite of the attempts
through the years
within various methods

~Keith Alan Hamilton~

moralizing and browbeating
our conversion
into the acceptance of
our responsibility
and recognition of our
inappropriate ways
by the offering of sacrifice
like our ancestors in the past
begging for appeasement
from the Nature gods
and forthwith
promising to change
by starting to live
more sustainably
and despite
all the denunciation
~   the earth
~ ~
let us pause
to let this following thought
sink in
become embedded
into our social character
~ ~
~   the earth
its environment,
its regulatory system
and the type of life
that will be able to survive
subjected to the earth's rules
the earth's way
is still going to change
again and again
regardless   ~
what humanity does
to realign its actions

Nature ~ I Q : Let's Survive, Not Die !

through rituals of obedience
and conformity
to this metaphorical
mother earth
or mythological Gaia
~ ~
let us then
We the people
change
what we can
by turning from
that cause of yesteryear
to the cause of today
may ~ may this
~ new cause
this
more ~ more
pertinent cause
be what is stood for,
marched for
and sung for
by the folk musician
let ~ let
the slogan of today
now become
more appropriately
~ Let's Survive, Not Die
let us ~ the proactive kind
speak to the people
protest in the streets
to tell
"The Man"
our servant
the government
what we expect
from its servitude

to help us,
help ourselves survive
by providing us
what we need
the foundation
and the vehicle
to do so ~
being more able to adapt
to earth change
~ for example,
making freely accessible
and affordable
to the people ~
~ an energy system
based on fission
and then overtime
transitioning to fusion
hence ~ proactively
being able to supply
the ever increasing demand
with a primary
and stable source
that can be supplemented
by other sustainable methods
helping to deter
any future chaotic turbulence
from occurring
within the populace
~ a transportation system
that would some day
include space travel
to population centers
boosting
the versatility
and efficiency of movement
for the people

Nature ~ I Q : Let's Survive, Not Die !

        making our time more useful
        and more capable
        in being beneficial to all
        ~ a health care system
        which will keep us
        fit, willing and able
        not only in body
        but mind
        assuring a wanting
        within the people
        for generations to come
        to keep trying to survive
        and to live on
        ~ an information/
        education system
        over a technology
        as the internet
        for a well rounded
        educated,
        perspective
        from a diversified
        free voice
        to stimulate curiosity
        and creativity
        possessed inside
        a wealth of ideas
        which will encourage
        an entrepreneurial spirit
        within the people
        ~ a housing system
        designed to provide
        a safe haven
        through novel innovation
        wherein ~ *able to adjust*
        its living environment
        to meet the effects

caused from earth change
and yet ~ a home
located within the hub
of a centralized community
giving all those
living in a neighborhood
a close proximity to all
that allows them
convenient access
to acquire and satisfy
their personal needs
~ 'cause then it would seem,
our servant
being utilized
to help provide
such a freely accessible
and affordable
living environment
humanity ~
would be assured the basis
for ongoing employment
a more stabilized economy
affording *the people*
more time and opportunity
to use our
clever
industriousness
spawned through
our creativity
and novel
inventiveness
to come up with
new and advanced
technologies
that could be implemented
in conjunction with

Nature ~ I Q : Let's Survive, Not Die !

primary and alternative
types of
contingency planning
that will be
and yes, should be
flexible
preparatory,
preventative
and transitional
enough in design
~ so to increase
our chances
of survival
through the ongoing process
of proactive adaptation
yes ~ the future survival
of you and me,
our families,
our children's
children's, children
that will makeup humanity
for generations to come
~ ~
~ 'cause
whether some
like it or not
fret for the sake of fretting
stomp their feet in resistance
yell foul
or blaspheme
and too, they'll be those
who won't be able
to alter
their activist mindset
colored with green
and yearning for peace

~Keith Alan Hamilton~

~ no matter the inhibitions
feeding the save the earth call
or the spiel,
humans deserve what they get
for what they've done
and the disclaimer,
why should I care,
I won't be alive then anyhow ~
humanity doesn't give a damn
why then try at all,
we're just gonna fail,
so let's live for the now
~ no matter the retort
the justified excuse,
out of mere necessity
caused by the eroding effects
of earth change
proactive humanity
including the activist
will fall in line for
call for ~
this 'new cause'
which will replace
"the cause" of old
where its slogan
"*Make Love, Not War*"
will become dead to the ear
as to the meaning of its voice
through the frantic
hustle and bustle
of *We the people* ~
crying aloud
around the world
resonating beyond the moon
to the stars
within the universe

31

Nature ~ I Q : Let's Survive, Not Die !

                as if the archangel
                in the book of Revelations
                crying out to "The Man"
                the government
                the servant of the people
                ~   help us now to prepare
                ~ *Let's Survive, Not Die*
                so our children born
                or yet to be born
                have the gift of life
                with a future   ~
                where they've become
                fully able
                aptly prepared
                and skilled to live on

if tomorrow comes
right attitude ~ mental adjustment

if tomorrow comes
be assured
I'll be ready   ~
to live on
ready as
the night watchman
waiting for the sun
to ascend
upon the horizon
~   whatever happens
I'll
rise up
early and eager
as the hoot   ~
of
the great horned owl
fades with the darkness
I'll
step forward
into the new day
as spry and agile
as   ~
that pronghorn deer
strutting its stuff
about the grassland
I   ~
have the right attitude
this wanting
to live for
work for
and fight for

Nature ~ I Q : Let's Survive, Not Die !

as the bear would do
to protect her cubs
~ I shall
do the same
for the future
of
not only me
my children
and their children's children
but for ~
the ongoing survival
of humanity
~ the human way
I must ~
I will
make the mental adjustment
despite the many sorrows
brewing
within the kettle
steaming over
with human apathy
which runs rampant
in the minds of those
held captive in a world
struggling
without hope
in a cause to live
day in and day out
that is not
built upon
the foundational pillars
of purpose
~ why
should I try ~
because
I

~Keith Alan Hamilton~

have to
it is inherent
to my nature
flowing
within my blood
as a species
learning to evolve
to survive
to go on
through the arrow
of time
~ what the hell else
a life ~
you and me
this living
all been for ~
life begets life
life then ~
lives on
emerging forth
the humankind
through you
and through me
 thus is a life
filled with purpose
with no need for guilt
or remorse
as the feeling of damnation
by a sin-ridden whore
not for ~
no ~ not at all for
those mistakes
we've made
or may continue to make
until we learn
from within a life of trying

Nature ~ I Q : Let's Survive, Not Die !

that process called   ~
intelligent progression

~ no way ~

screw those types
of feelings
to hell
with that
I say
there was no guidebook
~ if tomorrow comes
be assured
I'll be ready ~
to live on
and to help
my fellow human
do the same

~Keith Alan Hamilton~

~ to freely live
creating the way to do so

Roosevelt talked
of them
and then Rockwell
painted them
those four freedoms
noble goals
for humanity
to reach for   ~
well,
I think
we need
a little jolt first
like a jumpstart
to a car battery
a power of persuasion
that will
restart humanity
ignite the economy
getting us rolling
down the road
of life again
fueled on
by way of
five
freely
accessible
and affordable
resources
driving us forward
to better living
conditions   ~
and yet,

Nature ~ I Q : Let's Survive, Not Die !

for this kind of
road to be tread
for us to achieve
this promising
environment
its process
would need
to be supported,
implemented
and administered
by the servant
of the people
for the people
wherefore,
our government
creating the avenue
for making
freely accessible
and affordable
for all
and to all
a reliable
and primary
source for
~ *energy*
~ *information/*
education
~ *transportation*
~ *housing*
as well as
~ *health care*
all for   ~
keeping humanity
steady and strong
assuring a wanting
within the people

to live on   ~
therefore,
providing
the foundation,
the stimulus
for revitalizing
and creating jobs
to self-empower
We   ~
the people
into becoming
more of a contributor
as if the architect
laying out plans
to build our future
rather than
hopelessly the taker
walking the streets
forever
begging for
any handout
available
but instead,
within the struggle
of this process
similar to
the long distance
runner,
overcoming
the terrain
while heading for
the finish line
we create
together
for ourselves,
the possibility,

Nature ~ I Q : Let's Survive, Not Die !

        the opportunity
        to meet
        the expectations
        set before us
        in those four
        lofty goals
        ~ *freedom of speech*
        ~ *freedom of worship*
        ~ *freedom from want*
        and also
        ~ *freedom from fear*
        'cause we humans
        then,
        through our efforts
        will continue
        to survive
        from our ability
        ~   to freely live

~Keith Alan Hamilton~

Mother Earth: living our human way
letting go of the metaphorical mother

some people metaphorically call earth
mother, as in "Mother Earth"
or even in a more broader
all-encompassing sense, " Mother Nature"
now in Greek mythology
this mother nature was called, "Gaia"
no matter what analogy used
for some, the earth is portrayed
as if to be the giver and sustainer of life   ~
well if I may say so,
as a mother,
as a mother
like my real mother,
the earth as a mother
falls miserably short in the comparison
'cause my mother, although
genetically embodied
and socially embedded with human frailty
as a mom and a woman who has faced head on
many ills and obstacles set before her in life
as the mom who helped give me life
as the mom who helped sustain my life
who never, ever once allowed anything
affect or after undergoing the effect
of conditions thrust upon her
either directly or indirectly done to her
never, ever altered her role
as the giver and sustainer of my life
my mother has never, ever once
tried to bring harm to me or to
those daughters and sons of other mothers
my mother is a hero, even before

41

Nature ~ I Q : Let's Survive, Not Die !

I realized she would earn
such an honor beholden to my eyes
being felt way more
than some archetype of mind
emotionalized within my heart
oh mother earth, mother nature
the one known as this goddess Gaia,
I can't realistically or genuinely say or feel
nor conceptualize metaphorically
even begin to compare my Mother
my Mom or my Grandmother
as if ~ somehow ~ similar with you
however oh earth, well as if
you could actually hear and listen to me
I've come to know all too well
not only subjectively,
but objectively, I need to understand you
conceptualize beyond
the metaphors cast upon and over you
I must lift off the veil that shrouds
your role, your purpose, your function
within the scheme of all else
if not only for me, my children
and their children
also for humanity as a species
to be able to go on living
for us humans to be able to sustain
and preserve our kind into the future
must see you naked before me
the best I humanly can
without predisposition
being entrapped, ensnared
by any analogy, symbolism or belief
subtly fogging, biasing
or impeding my judgment
as to clearly seeing, perceiving

~Keith Alan Hamilton~

and fully envisioning
what you are now or may come to be
whether as to your worth
or out of mere necessity to detach from you
~ oh earth, despite your changes
uncovered in the past or yet to happen
even if drastically disruptive changes
that may occur within or upon you
like rapid and destabilizing climate change,
with violent weather, as well as global plagues,
super-volcanoes or killer asteroids from the sky,
earthquakes or tsunamis
or human born nuclear war or terrorism   ~
even the arrival of
unfriendly extraterrestrials, etc.
I hold no malice or blame against you
for you know not what you do
as a planet or portion that is only a sub-system
a dynamic part of a whole system
undergoing complex activities
the holomovement as explained by Bohm,
recurrent patterns of process
energy/matter
unfolding and enfolding
interacting, interconnecting
and being interdependent as
the living and the nonliving
the animate and the inanimate
as manifested in the physical reality
which comprises in its totality ~ Nature
nor earth, as I learn about you
and all else as aspects within Nature
do I hold any malice for or blame
against my kind, the humankind
'cause we evolved upon you through survival
sheer willpower we used, even while dying

Nature ~ I Q : Let's Survive, Not Die !

no manual or guidebook to follow
only living and trying
by way of self-production, variation
cooperation and adaptation
eventually, attempting to pass on
information in the form of
knowledge and wisdom
as much as what was learned
from our struggle within thought
comprehended or imagined along the way
to survive, we've had to move on,
regardless of the happenings of the past
and yes at times,
in spite of how things were
may have seemingly always been
we've had to let go of
our metaphors
traditions, our symbolism
and our beliefs held so tightly
with all their comforts
we've left them behind, forever
as nothing but memories of our past
~
yes one day, oh Mother Earth,
Mother Nature, the Greek goddess Gaia
the regulator of our human lives
even though,
in a metaphorically sense
you are a poor
and inadequate mother to the humankind
holding us captive to your systemic ways
if humanity is going to survive, go on
we'll have to free ourselves
partially or wholly from your
archetypical bondage
like any loving mother

~Keith Alan Hamilton~

you'll have to let us use our wings
to fly among and throughout the stars
that expanded environment
of Nature's totality
holding out hope
within the human mind
at present littered with inhibition and guilt
you must completely without remorse
let us go ~
so finally we'll more fully learn
from the opportunity of having the chance
to move about unencumbered,
as an embryonic child
detached at birth from the mother's womb
after cutting the tie of the umbilical cord
casting behind once and for all
the hindrance preventing us ~
limiting us from living our human way

Nature ~ I Q : Let's Survive, Not Die !

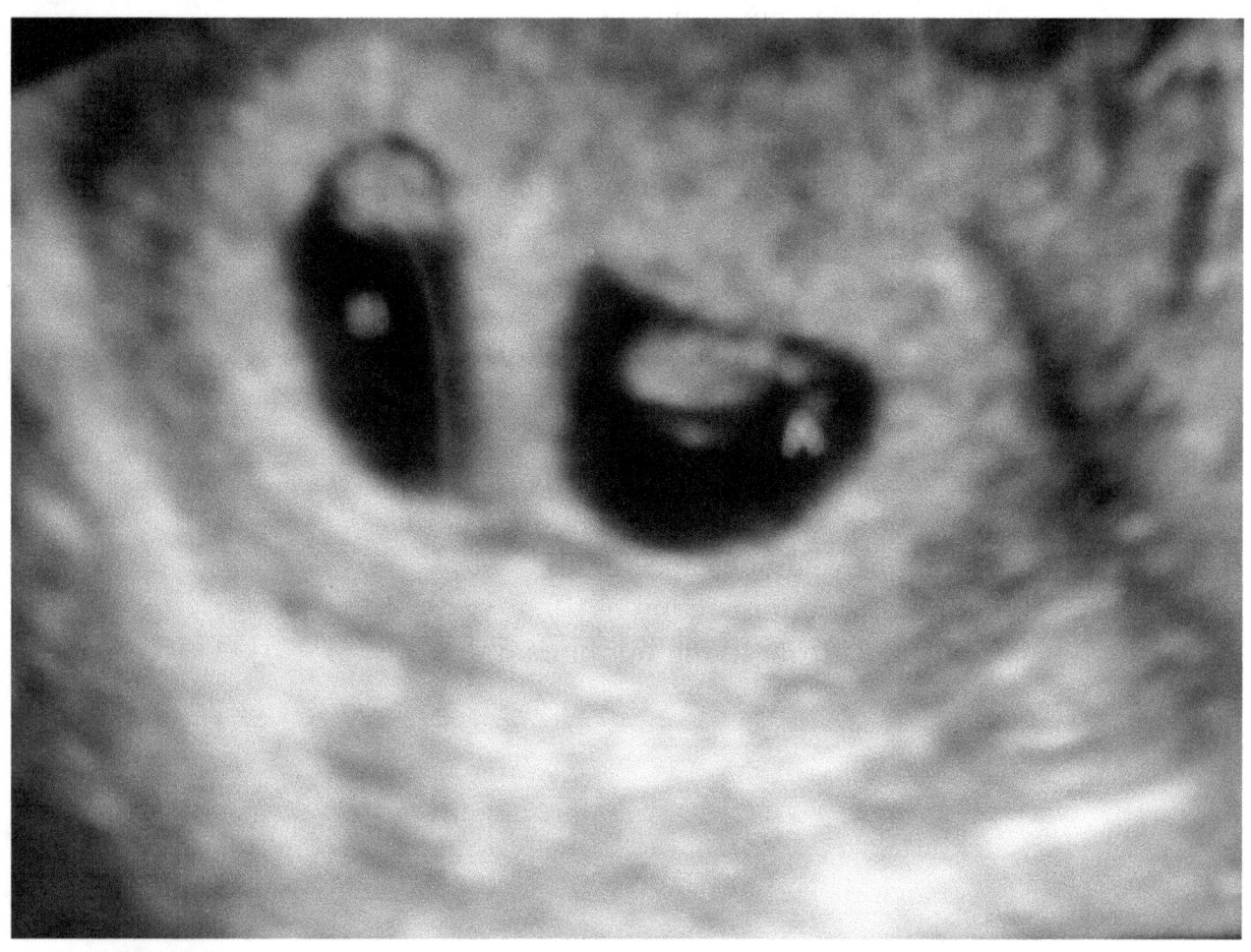

my fellow humans
let's get beyond it all.....

ok my fellow humans
not going to sit around
wallowing in the past
all forlorn acting and stuff
bitching about
way back whenever
how much simpler
more so-called natural times
were somehow, someway
the best way and the only way
 ~   really my fellow humans
really, I don't care
or give a damn
about the blame game
who was right,
who were wrong
could of   ~   would of
should of
lived sustainably
consumed less things
stopped having so many babies
been more leery of technology
industrialization
economic development
the perils of capitalism
like somehow the sprawl
the waste of humanity
succeeding and enjoying life
eating and shitting
are the acts of the evil sort
or some evolutionary plight
destine for the ignoramus

Nature ~ I Q : Let's Survive, Not Die !

~ listen my fellow humans
sure we should live
then learn from the past
sure it is wise to know
what happen
when we did this or that
the result of it all
not just by or to ourselves
but with and to each other
~ however
my fellow humans
come on now
how presumptuous
within the complexity of it all
you and me
the well-educated
the intellectual
that scientist
that environmentalist
some preacher or prophet
or some extraterrestrial
have become so smart
so all knowing
that they or someone
can now conceive
conceptualize
see what is
see how it should be
as to foresee
enough to change
enough to alter
the arrow of time
perform the act
of reversibility
as if to turn back the clock
back to when some thought

~Keith Alan Hamilton~

life was intended to be
where all of Nature
should of somehow, someway
always forevermore
stayed as they remembered
as they seen it fit
or simply wanted it to be
~   adapt my fellow humans
let's not waste our moments
judging and romancing the past
~   forward in time
let's get beyond it all.....
not just for ourselves
but for the sake
of our children's children
for the preservation of our kind
so future generations
won't waste time
bitching and moaning
about our laxity
our inability
to live for the future
squandering away
our lives and lives to come
on some way it was back when
which will never
without question
come to pass,
repeat in the exact manner
to recreate someone's memory
~   rather my fellow humans
may our example
our proactive ways
be what's remembered
where the hindsight learned
as to generations to become

Nature ~ I Q : Let's Survive, Not Die !

embody the foresight
that's embedded
with our efforts
that our inhibitions to let go
held with white knuckled fear
did not consume us
prevent us from using
our mind
with clever industriousness
spawned by our creativity
novel inventiveness
to mold and to develop
come up with those
new and advanced
technologies
implemented along with
primary and alternative
contingency planning
that may increase
our chances for survival
not only
needing to be flexible
but also preparatory,
preventative
and transitional in design
which will then overcome
~ spit in the eye
resisting all those forces
systemically forcing
our kind to accept its demise

someway ~ somehow
we shall go on

the water will rise from global heating

revealing the womb of our evolution

turning its tide against us ~ the earth system

has a so-called tipping point ~

not unlike the *Leaning Tower of PIZA*

in spite of what we do ~ or try

the foundational pattern stabilizing the climate

will change ~ no longer staying the way it is

or go back to the way we want it to be

this rising of seas will force humanity

to migrate inland as the many birds of the air

have done so regularly for centuries

a learned migration ~ caused by a change of season

the humankind though ~ unlike the bird

can't so easily relocate ~ 'cause of being attached

to a home with family and many possessions

but will learn through adaptation to seek out

dry land not overrun by the persistent waters

and yet ~ before the time for such a happening

Nature ~ I Q : Let's Survive, Not Die !

we humans ~ humbly must admit our ignorance
about how the great earth system works
come to accept that living green ~ planting trees
reducing our carbon footprint ~ blaming ourselves
is not enough ~ even if motivated by noble intentions
we won't be able to reverse Nature's fervent march
acting as if some military brigade of old
drumming out the beat of its advancement
one step after another ~ pushing straight ahead
for an unalterable climax called climate change
therefore ~ despite such a grim prognosis
humanity must prepare to adapt to the onslaught
focus wholeheartedly on the most pertinent things
intelligently plan ahead ~ invoke the human spirit
respond accordingly and appropriately to the threat
so the human race ~ our children's children
as in the past and hopefully into the future
we shall go on ~ grow up and then prosper
continue to survive ~ someway ~ somehow

humankind acts in a way
a more aware ~ way of being

the humankind acts in a way
and it's ~   not so much
~   as if it's
this matter of sin
associated with imperfection
the doing of right and wrong
based on following or breaking
some moral code
etched on stone tablets
by God   ~   for us humans
or the lacking of intelligence
'cause of inadequate
circuitry development
along the evolutionary path
due to DNA
and socially embedded
survival imprints
within the larval/yokel brain
as expounded by Leary
and further propagated by RAW
~   however
humanity does act in a way
emulating this pattern for living
struggling to stay alive
as observed in Nature
very similar to ~
the many other kinds of life
moving about upon a planet

Nature ~ I Q : Let's Survive, Not Die !

holding them as captives
beginning with birth
without the liberty of choice
and inalienable rights
as is more powerfully illustrated
and therefore ~ taken to heart
by conceptualizing within mind
the cruel and uncivilized activity
revealed through human slavery
~ where in like manner
all life is forcefully subjected
to the rules of land ~ sea and air
within the regulatory process
of the figurative ~ lording master
Gaia ~ so-called Mother Earth
~ thus is such
and in a way ~
humanity
does appear rather busy
eking out a daily existence
caring for a family
with needs and desires
sort of like
the past behavior
remember ~ those people
portrayed in the biblical story
about Noah and the ark
~ similarly today
We the people don't fully realize
completely take notice
or pay attention to
nor think much about

not even ~ wanting
to envision metaphorically
what's told through tales as history
about the great flood of old
synonymous in many ways to ~
the encroaching waters
on the horizon
from melting sheets of ice
~ ice melt
rising water levels
regardless of
what or who is the reason
from a global heating
predicted to worsen
according to the modern day
prophets
~ born again
with the Holy Spirit of Science
fervently forecasting
disruptive changes will occur
within the workings
of the earthly system
and yet or maybe after
as the earth system sage
the Gaian spiritual leader
James Lovelock has said ~
if humankind is going to finally
take note ~ get serious
it will be when
one of the major glaciers
in the west of Antarctica
does melt away as a popsicle

Nature ~ I Q : Let's Survive, Not Die !

left out on a warm summer day
finally suffers a total collapse
no doubt   ~   this sort of happening
will raise sea levels
just enough to forcefully
coerce humanity
into a more heightened
more aware   ~   way of being
focusing thinking on ways
more concerned with survival
~   for example
"*proactive adaptation planning*"
so the humankind   ~
if bestowed a blessing
from Father Time
~   is given enough time
to prepare   ~   as if
readying fortifications
setting battle formations
before the onslaught of war
concentrating beforehand
upon the right things
those pertinent and pressing
conditions that have been
bequeathed our immediate
and undivided attention
affording us the opportunity
to develop the capabilities
giving us the ability to adjust
for and then from ~   the impact
~   'cause
the rising seas   ~   the waters

will inundate coastal areas
places along the river's edge
flooding and eroding the lands
seeping into every nook and cranny
destabilizing building foundations
creating sinkholes   ~   which
all together   ~   will threaten
the people   ~   the biodiversity
of cities   ~   small and large
throughout the world
~   wherefore
increasing public health risk
altering patterns of weather
becoming harsher   ~   producing
stronger tornadoes and hurricanes
bringing forth more tidal waves
spreading the perils of drought
even weakening   ~   an already
inadequately resourced   ~
overly taxed   ~   national security
emergency preparedness
and crisis management system
~   for instance
at the present
if several coastal cities
were besieged by the waters
and then while languishing
within this diminished state
the nature gods   ~   show no mercy
willfully   ~   smiting the downtrodden
blasting them with
some angry hurricane

Nature ~ I Q : Let's Survive, Not Die !

or with the twisting winds
driving on a hostile tornado
the people of America
couldn't even adequately
care for their own
let along stop the borders
from being over run
by opportunistic marauders
as if to be stampeded with
frenzied herds of spooked cattle
while trying to deal with the chaos
that would surely follow
~ in all humility
if hardly able ~
to care for themselves
how possibly
under such conditions
even if dubiously labeled
"the superpower"
how could America lend
a helping hand to other nations
facing similar situations
throughout the world
especially ~ if ill-prepared
~ for is it not the chaos
that would ensue
from a grief stricken
and panicked people
with no plan ~ with no hope
pilfering about in an all out
survival mode
the greatest force to fear

~Keith Alan Hamilton~

the biggest threat to demoralizing
the human spirit
and to breaking down
the infrastructure of a society
~ would it be not better
to prepare for ~
the most crucial challenges
facing humankind today
even if ~ we may not solve them
or stop them ~ but only hinder
the progression of them ~ just enough
so humanity ~ our children
can be given more time
maybe then ~ working out
how to be able to better adapt
in the future and more able
to figure out what's next to do
by providing them and us
through previous preparation
the golden opportunity
to learn during the experience
what are the most important things
that need to be done
together ~ cooperatively as one
rather than through a disoriented state
fractured ~ fighting against
and deterring one another
living some hysterical ~ chaotic hell
~ regardless of what
Gaia ~ Mother Earth
the nature gods may cast down
rise up ~ blow or spread about

upon land ~ out of sea
or over air
while increasing our torment
under the heat of the sun
if the humankind can act in a way
that's preemptive ~ through
"proactive adaptation planning"
focusing our attention
improving our national security
emergency preparedness
and crisis management system
~ around readying ourselves
for whatever earth changes
that are to come ~ especially
those that will rise our waters
only to severely impact
and alter our way of life
yes ~ *We the people* together
the humankind ~
can and will adapt
by taking the time now
to learn what we should do
then do it the best we can
~ *Let's Survive, Not die*
through preparation
triumphantly securing
our children ~
our children's children
a life that has a lasting future
filled with the purpose to live on
from knowing the legacy
by following the example

~Keith Alan Hamilton~

left by our generation
~ being that
humankind acted in a way
they prepared while living
facing head on ~ focusing upon
the most crucial ~
most threatening
~ challenges
at the right time
which could have destabilized
the infrastructure of the people
bringing about
the self-destructive
forces of chaos
so then ~ today
here and now
henceforth ~
humanity as a whole
most keep fighting
amidst the struggle
never become apathetic
never give up
or helplessly
throw our hands in the air
as if defeated
but ~ always ~ always
keep trying ~ despite
what ominously approaches
upon the horizon ~ no matter
how bleak the circumstance
may seem ~

~ there will be a tomorrow
worthy ~ of us fighting for

Nature ~ I Q : Let's Survive, Not Die !

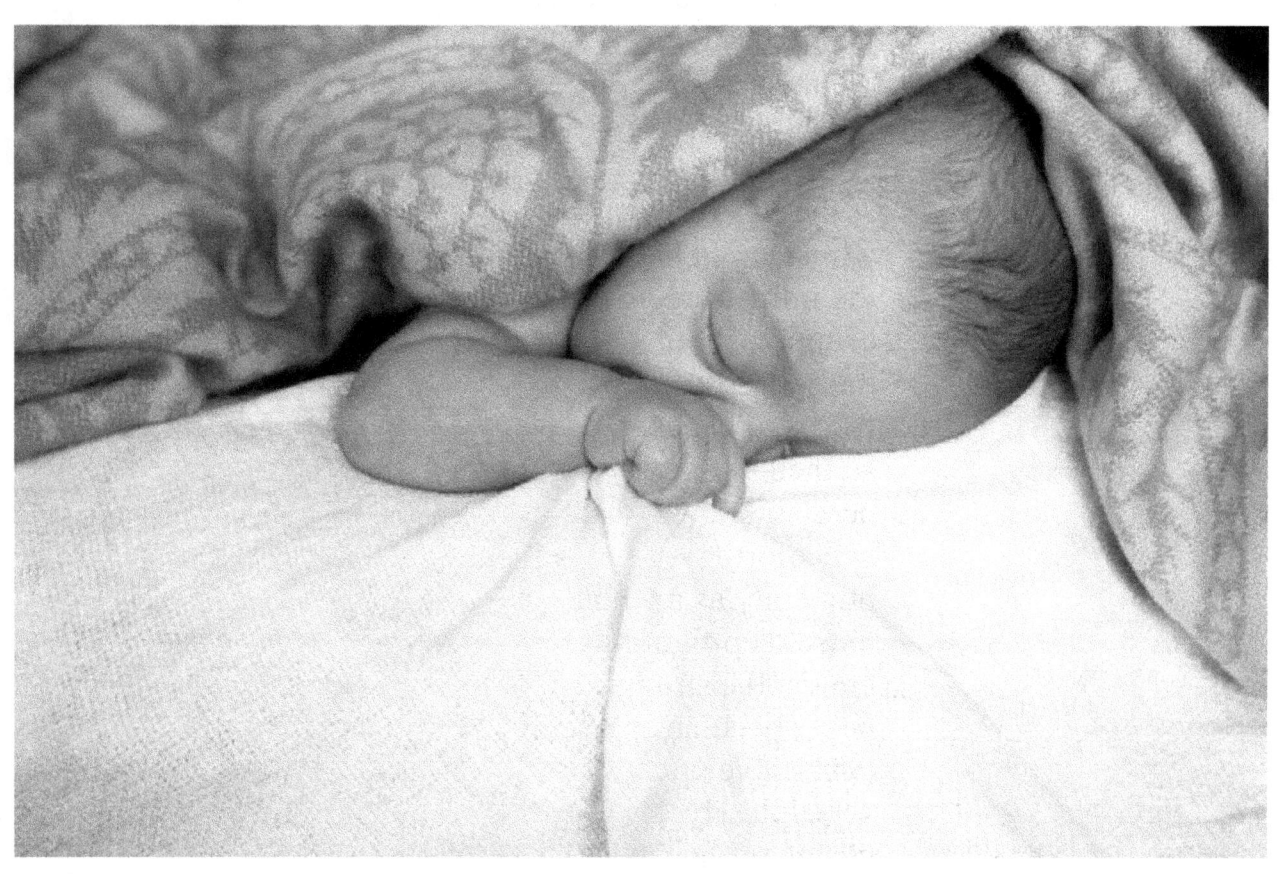

Photography by Jenna Lindberg

~Keith Alan Hamilton~

a new ~ Independence Day
against all odds

within a revolution
of the people
blood ~ gore
and some
spirited determination
We the people
with a little help
from other nations
freed ourselves
our families ~ neighbors
and friends
against all odds
from the tyranny
of the crown
birthing a new nation
the United States
as remembered yearly
on *Independence Day*
and yet ~ while
jubilantly celebrating
the anniversary
of our freedom
our release from servitude
We the people
still are willing
to tolerate despotism
~ feel comfortable
with enslavement
of our people

Nature ~ I Q : Let's Survive, Not Die !

          even after ~
          measures were taken
          to cleanse ourselves
          of slavery's mentality
          and the ill manner
          within herding
          Native American people
          as bison into the lands
          designated for captivity
          but yet ~ while
          living the experience
          this transitional period
          of an intelligently
          progressive ~
          learning process
          We the people
          have naturally accepted
          amidst the ways
          bestowed by
          social conditioning
          from the elements
          ~ those same limitations
          imposed on
          our rights for choice ~
          mandates levied
          upon our present
          and potential liberty
          yes ~ our incarceration
          inside environmental
          conditions ~ using
          the centrifugal
          gravitational forces

under the premise
proclaimed as being
laws of nature
to stake out
its boundary
for an oxygenated
bubble dome
our prison
called earth ~ which
when pondered
~ its formation
is not so unlike
that of a once was
monarchy that unjustly
empowered the crown
of King George III
~ Nature
~ the totality
of all energy/matter
the living
and the nonliving
by way of the laws
enforced by its
nature gods
within a despotic
earth system ~ does tax
the life choices
of *all the people*
through drastically
disruptive change
within the workings of its
regulatory process

Nature ~ I Q : Let's Survive, Not Die !

therefore ~
like in the past
will eventually motivate
within a revolution
of the people
blood ~ gore
and some
spirited determination
We the people
with a little help
from other nations
shall free ourselves
our families ~ neighbors
and friends
against all odds
from the tyranny
of Nature's
earthly crown
birthing a new
way of living
with a liberty reaching
beyond the constraints
imposed by earth
to the stars
as then ~
remembered yearly
on a new ~
Independence Day

if we say ~ peace
is our protest enough

if we say ~ peace
protest about it
wear t-shirts
marked with its symbol
display it on
banners and signs
unify it by a march
through the streets
~ so
the people ~
the man ~
the servant ~
the government
~ of
the people
~ for
the people
may observe
and listen
to our plea ~
our hope and prayer
filled with expectation
a desire for our children
our children's children
to live in a world
free of violence
void of despair

Nature ~ I Q : Let's Survive, Not Die !

~   and yet
is our protest enough
being all that's needed
for change   ~
for peace   ~

~ *FUCK NO* ~

if peace
is gonna happen
the people
must do more
way   ~   way
much   ~   much more
is needed
then walk and talk
finger pointing
and that blame game
~   *the people*
not from just one nation   ~
gender   ~
race
or way of belief
~   but more of
the people
the better   ~   as one
must work together
cooperatively
and industriously

properly utilizing
the man ~
the servant ~
the government
~ of
the people
~ for
the people
to come up with a plan
plot out a course
based on concepts
and ideals
that are
proactive enough ~
flexible enough ~
transitional enough
and driven by enough
innovative technology
~ so to
create
an environment
of betterment ~
joy from prosperity
which ~ overall
shall improve upon
the physical ~
the mental
and social wellbeing
of *the people*
among *the people*
everywhere ~
throughout the earth

~   then the tendency
the behavior of *the people*
fueled by jealousy
and hatred
encouraged from
lack and want
that feeds
violence and restricts
the *process of peace*
will change
'cause *the people*
from helping *the people*
help themselves
not so unlike the captain
equipped with modern
navigational concepts
and technology
confidently steers
a ship through
the turbulent sea
the people can and will
successfully reach
in the future
those calm waters
of *peace*   ~
if we say   ~   *peace*
protest about it
wear t-shirts
marked with its symbol
display it on
banners and signs
unify it by a march

through the streets
~ so
the people ~
the man ~
the servant ~
the government
~ of
the people
~ for
the people
may observe
and listen
to our plea ~
~ well then
let us *the people*
support
what it will take
to bring about
such a happening
the very things
that will cause
peace to become
for *the people* ~

~ freely accessible
an affordable
energy ~
information/education ~
transportation ~
health care
and housing

peace out ~ *people*

begin to heal ourselves
responsible for our destiny

from the bottom of my heart
with every ounce
of my soul ~ my spirit
yearns for
world healing
peace   ~
equality
and prosperity
for *the people*
by *the people*
is the only way
such a happening
will ever come to be

~ simply said
but not so
easy to do ~

~ *We the people*
all as individuals
uniquely contributing
our gift ~
our willpower
working together
cooperatively
and steadfastly
with a purpose   ~
are the architects
the initiators
the idea creators
the planners

~Keith Alan Hamilton~

the laborers
the result makers
responsible for our destiny

~   'cause
that's the way it is
in Nature   ~   the physical
there ain't no shortcuts
nor some quick fix   ~

~   our thoughts
our voices through word
and art   ~
can and will raise
social awareness

~   have an effect upon
collective consciousness
and yet   ~
our thoughts
our words
are not enough
with thought and word
there needs to be   ~
the act   ~   the deed
the no quit attitude
and determination

Nature ~ I Q : Let's Survive, Not Die !

~   despite
the perceived
the feared
insurmountable
can't see beyond
the struggle
the hate
the greed
the violence
the intolerance
the bias
the inequality
the suffering
type of conditions
those odds
standing in the way
of attaining the prize
blurring our ability
to bring change   ~

~   if we want
world healing
peace   ~
equality
and prosperity
for *the people*
by *the people*
then you and I
through word and thought
acts   ~   deeds
must make it come to be   ~

~ *We the people*
humanity
must create a world
to help ourselves
thus *as one*
together
cooperatively
let us
bring about
the environment
to do so   ~
support the development
through innovative ideas
and technologies
a freely accessible
and affordable
~   energy source
~   information/
education
~   transportation
~   housing
and health care

~   so humanity can start
begin
to heal
ourselves
then afterwards   ~
the world
and possibly beyond

Nature ~ I Q : Let's Survive, Not Die !

surviving earth change
choose for life

looming in our future
are super-volcanoes, killer asteroids
global plagues, climate change,
et cetera
all could bring to fruition
disruptive variations of earth change ~
what will we do about these threats
give up, give in,
as well as feel guilty
about what
should of ~ could of
been done
therefore resigning ourselves over
to pity's burden and apathy's reign

some say don't worry, there's really
nothing we can do; why not ignore it
and if such things would happen at all
it's doubtful it'll occur during our life

others on high infer,

we them masses ain't
smart enuff to change nuttin
and us peoples
no ways gonna change,
'cause we keep doin'
like we always do

"*you can take that to the ban*k"

~Keith Alan Hamilton~

well ~ in spite of
what the politician
or even some preacher
or that
well-educated intellectual
and scientist claim ~   I say
bull-pucky,
just yous wait a sec
and in the way my common,
everyday grandpa used to say,
*"yous pert near had me a thinkin'
in a way, heaped full of feelings
and paralyzing fears"*
I nearly forgot about sound reason

just because the *THEY*
say it is so
doesn't mean
all things said by *THEM*
are right or is
the only way to follow
or become   ~
and the hell
with that screwed up
guilt trip thing
living is hard enough
to waste energy
on the blame game
pointing our finger
at one another

Nature ~ I Q : Let's Survive, Not Die !

let us use
our mind to reason
let's use
our ability to question

who gave us humans
some kind of guidebook
revealing every step of the way
about living
that would guarantee
our ongoing survival
come on now
we gotta stay open-minded
about the facts
what was
how it happened
as experienced
when we and those
of the past lived them

let us think
and let's remember

didn't *We the people*
do what   ~
what we had too
didn't we survive, live adaptively
humanizing our chances by novelty
creatively bettering our lives
through much toil, blood, sweat
and yes through tears

~Keith Alan Hamilton~

not just as other life
with pure brawn
where the strong
shall survive
but we also
used our brain
which is so, so fully
demonstrated
by way of our technology ~
like in the past, so in the future
We the people
can and will survive
earth changes
if we want too ~
if *We the people*
work in a proactive way
struggle
through tireless effort
within our shared
thinking process
not so unlike, we humans
have had to do
so many times in the past
even if different
regarding the circumstances ~

if *We the people*
face it head on
determined to go on
despite
whatever
the earth change
presenting itself before us

Nature ~ I Q : Let's Survive, Not Die !

we together,
you and me
within our cooperative
lived experience
sharing a common purpose
of survival
pressing on as one
a proactive oneness
emerging a *sort of*
spiritual bond
spirited on
by the connectivity
of our interactions
our interrelationships
illuminating the benefit
embedded into
our interdependence
inherently
embodied ~
entwined
into our evolutionary
process of life
that desire to live on ~
survive
no matter what ~
if *We the people*
help each other
and then within such a spirit
if *We the people*
by way of our cooperative acts
engaging the help of our government
partnering together ~

~Keith Alan Hamilton~

create a more freely accessible
and affordable living environment
a living environment shaped around
proven concepts and practices
those of energy ~
information/education ~
transportation ~
health care and housing ~
concepts and practices
which create employment ~
satisfy supply and demand ~
stabilize the economy ~
inhibiting chaotic conditions
from materializing within *the people*
wherein ~ along the way
during the lived experience
of such a cooperative process
that of human betterment
and empowerment
while expanding our *Nature ~ IQ*
We the people
can give birth to
intelligently perceptive insights
insights,
intelligently applied
with innovative technologies

if *We the people*
mutually ~ within an
intelligently progressive
learning process
yes ~ we together,
you and me

learning to implement
our insights with technology
in conjunction with *proactive*
primary and alternative
contingency planning
contingency plans
needing to be *preparatory,*
preventative, flexible
and transitional
just the right amount of ~
mitigation and adaptation
scientifically
formulated around
a more holistic understanding
of the universal processes
regulating all Nature
as a whole system
not just the earth ~

~ for instance
just an example
if we prepare now to adapt
by focusing on the right things
when climate change occurs
laying fallow our fields
our so-called bread basket
a land of waste
from the effect of draught
we convert the land
letting go of its
once thought of purpose
planting

no longer tilled rows
with seeds of solar panels
providing then   ~
a supplemental energy source
which would grow
permanent jobs around
operation and maintenance
feeding the economy
keeping it stable
helping to satisfy
supply and demand
while helping to prevent
blackouts and shortages
within the primary
source of energy
in the process of evolving
from fission to fusion

~   and in like mind
producing similar results
how 'bout
a self-sustaining
Bucky Fuller type
geodesic dome-housing
for the people
to live and prosper
becoming more resilient
to the drastically disruptive
effects of whatever
manifestation of earth change

Nature ~ I Q : Let's Survive, Not Die !

                even if ~ such abodes
                due to a changing environment
                need to be constructed
                and transitionally adjusted
                redesigned to fit
                the current circumstance
                upon or below the land
                above or within the waters
                or in the sky
                or if necessary
                orbiting the earth
                and even beyond
                offering an alternative option
                for an ever-expanding populace
                overflowing with opportunity
                and adventure that could lend to
                the preservation   ~
                the survival of our kind

                wherefore ~
                within the mitigation
                and even more so
                the *proactive adaptation*
                of *We the people*
                partnering with our government
                to reinvent, create and develop
                concepts and practices
                like these……

~Keith Alan Hamilton~

beholden to the hope
and the faith
within the spirit for life
we can and shall survive
somehow, somewhere
even if, all seemingly
above and beyond
so far from what
we together,
you and me
may now know
but still, right there
before us all
to fight for and obtain

only if ~
We the people ~ humanity
choose not only to live
we together ~ you and me
should also *choose for life*
offering our children and their
children's children
the choice to live and go on

Conclusion

The subtitle of the poem Beyond 2012 in this book's introduction says: gonna be more proactive. Hopefully, *We the people* will feel the urgency, the need to make the choice to be more proactive about the drastically disruptive earth change lurking on the horizon. If so, *We the people* must then begin to communicate clearly in a nonpartisan manner our united ideas, beliefs, hopes and dreams beyond the activist marching in the street. This type of communication process would embrace novel thinking aligned appropriately by using innovative technology. Such a communicative process should also be wisely integrated with proven concepts and practices within the social/economic areas of energy, information/education and transportation, housing and health care. These concepts and practices should serve the objective of being implemented as freely accessible and affordable to all of *We the people*. Yes, freely accessible and affordable resources that will uplift the spirit of *We the people* by creating an environment that enhances our wellbeing and prosperity. An improved mental and physical condition overall, where *We the people* are more willing and able to help ourselves and others to endure whatever humanity has to overcome. Concepts and practices that are put together as part of a process, a process that's stabilizing, resilient, and transitional by being more forward thinking in perspective. A process strategically planned that uses methods of mitigation. However recognizes the need for it to be more reliant on the methods of proactive adaptation because of properly deducing the time and circumstance. Overall it will be a proactively planned strategy for the betterment of humanity, as well as the ongoing survival of, *We the people*.

If such a united and nonpartisan process of communication is to begin between *We the people* and our servant(s), the government(s) on a global scale, the following would need to occur:

- *We the people* must come to understand that the Nature ~ IQ of humanity regarding the earth's regulatory system for life to live (including climate) is minimal at best. We do not know enough to even start to fix the earth's now destabilizing regulatory system. We cannot first save the earth to save ourselves. *We the people* must first learn to save ourselves, and then within the adaptive struggle to do so, we may learn ways to save other living aspects of the earth as well.

- With drastically disruptive earth change approaching, combined with our lack of knowledge about the great earth system, *We the people* need to spend less time on mitigation practices and more time on developing the concept and strategies associated with *proactive adaptation planning*. Is not the adaptive struggle within the process of evolution humankind's strong suit? Our ability to be cognitively aware, evaluate our interaction with our surroundings and then within this process of reflective consciousness we intelligently progress, learn from our experiences. As in our evolutionary past, the human species, *We the people* can creatively evolve ways to save ourselves, even though it will take much effort and struggle to think together to do so.

- Despite humankind's difference of opinion, our diverse array of beliefs, traditions, cultures, national ideology, political parties, etc., if our overall purpose is focused on one key goal, the survival of humanity, then we can set aside our difference of opinion. *We the people* together, working with our servant(s) the government(s) can then communicate more freely, unencumbered without bias or hidden agenda. Globally together, *We the people* and our government(s) can form a nonpartisan collective; a think tank so to speak, to figure out how to adapt to, and then survive drastically distributive earth change. This collective mindset could then be used as one voice to communicate clearly and effectively to *We the people*, the humankind throughout the world, what needs to be done.

Nature ~ I Q : Let's Survive, Not Die !

- To be successful, to be able to survive as a species, *We the people* of the planet are going to have to adapt and alter our overall perspective about Nature's earth and its changing regulatory system, especially about what we are used to experiencing in the world's climate. In reality, archetypically or metaphorically, this so-called Gaia, the earth, is not our loving mother, or even a concerned friend. The earth does not have the consciousness to ascertain or discern conditions properly and then judge humanity fairly when it comes to our species' ongoing future. Systemically the earth like Nature as a whole is not partial or caring towards humanity when it comes to the regulation of its ways, the sustainability of its dynamic patterns of climate during human times. It would be better, far wiser to perceive earth from a human perspective for what it is, a conscienceless slave master restricting our freedom and the scope of our ability to survive. How so you may ask? By encapsulating humanity within a centrifugally gravitated, atmospherically oxygenated-bubble dome prison. If anything, as the earth system becomes more drastically disruptive, with more erratic changes to what once was a more stable, cyclical climate pattern (where humanity has evolved and thrived), the earth system will behaviorally act more like a terrorist, a heartless warmonger. Why you may ask? As the earth destabilizes its patterns of climate that provided an environment suitable for humanity, it will cause havoc on the overall planetary ecosystem, including the infrastructure that sustains human society. Its actions through more violent weather, expanding draught, rising earth's waters, migrating life to adjust, etc., will instill fear, and then through panic will provoke chaos spreading through the populace. Earth the terrorist becomes the heartless warmonger. Its acts through earth change creates the potential to destroy the very fabric binding humanity as a species together from within, through ourselves. Drastically disruptive earth change will pressure human to turn against human and other life to fight for mere survival, without remorse for doing so on the earth's part.

- Besides changing our perception of the earth and seeing its drastically disruptive changes for what they are, *We the people* need to accept humanity for who we are and what we will become in the years to come. First, *We the people* need to shed the guilt for being simply human, for making mistakes while learning from our experiences. We need to quit blaming each other for the human role of contributing to drastically disruptive earth change. Wasting our time on such emotion-filled pursuits, centered on a knowledge extremely lacking as to how the earth system really works and what would contribute to changing it, is not only fruitless but counterproductive to our ongoing survival. We were not given an all-encompassing guidebook listing specific, step by step details as to how the earth system works and how we could prevent our effect on the earth as we evolved and populated it. Humanity is not aware of the many hidden factors as to why the earth's regulatory system and its climate are now changing. Humanity cannot even perceive these changes objectively. As the Permian period of the earth's history millions of years ago is starting to reveal, drastically disruptive earth change and climate change were not caused back then by one factor as life living life (mammal-like reptiles), but by many contributing factors. Second, *We the people* cannot let the immensity of the earth system and its powerful ability to drastically disrupt the climate as we know it, overwhelm us. It is not wrong to be human, have children and to eat, drink and be merry. It is not a sin to be pro-human, to proactively fight against the terrorist, warmongering earth for the ongoing survival of humanity. It is not wrong for humans to create and to improve the overall condition of *We the people,* make the tools to do so freely accessible and affordable to everyone. So the human spirit will become uplifted, to better our wellbeing by helping ourselves and others to survive. It is not wrong to raise the confidence in our abilities to improve our Nature ~ IQ and find ways to preserve our kind, fight the odds against us despite the forces of earth. It is not wrong to be proactive, plan to adapt, transition and transform our lives like the butterfly, where *We the people*, our children and our children's children will live on and on, even if for some of us, it's beyond the captivity of the earth.

Nature ~ I Q : Let's Survive, Not Die !

a clear cut message
communicate it to all ~

We the people
who want change
~ change to improve
the wellbeing
of humanity
those of us
who want
to be able to survive
into the future
must become prepared
speak up ~
and become part
of the process
not wait around
put all our trust
and our hope
in our elected servant
our government
but *We the people*
need to think of ~
bring forth ways
for the people
to more readily face
and then adapt to
whatever
obstacles
Nature
and its earth
sets before us
~ *We the people*
need to have ~
have to develop

~Keith Alan Hamilton~

a clear cut message
and then ~
we must
proactively
communicate it to all ~
all who will listen
yes ~ a message
that lays out
our ideas
based on
well thought-out
and proven
concepts and practices
concepts and practices
even if ~
not all new
however ~
made to be more
forward thinking
than when applied
in the past
therein ~
more able to meet
the needs
of the people
now
and of the people
who are yet to come
concepts and practices
similar to those put forth by
Alexander Hamilton
that stimulated
the growth of
a new nation
which helped the people
help themselves

Nature ~ I Q : Let's Survive, Not Die !

to live and to prosper
~ *We the people*
of today
within the spirit of
cooperation
can do the same
if *We the people*
become willing to form
a partnership
with the servant
of the people
for the people
our appointed
representative
not to create
another way of doing things
as far as
our basic ideals
of liberty
and commerce
by creating some
overly dependent
socialist/communist
ideology
or some
welfare state
absent of
free enterprise
and self-responsibility
nor ~
somehow again
over-empowering
the government
where despotism
has free reign
but rather

~Keith Alan Hamilton~

we together
with our servant
need to bring forth
well thought-out
and proven
concepts and practices
that will fuel
and encourage
the growth of
private enterprise
within the areas of ~
~ energy
~ information/
education
~ transportation
~ housing
and health care
concepts and practices
that most of all
will make these areas
of focus ~

freely accessible
and affordable
to all the people
designed and implemented
in conjunction
with the benefits
found in technology

~ listen please
once again
I'll reiterate ~

Nature ~ I Q : Let's Survive, Not Die !

concepts and practices
that remain favorable
to the people's way
which maintain
the proper balance
between the rights
and values of the people
and the amount
of assistance provided
by their servant
concepts and practices
that stay flexible
and transitional
enough to meet
the people's needs
in the present
and the days to come
through a mindset
that's proactive
and adaptive

why ~
'cause to
help the people
to be fit ~
ready
and able
become more resilient
and self-sufficient
more able
to carry on
with everyday life
especially so ~
being more prepared
to endure
to survive

any type of
drastically disruptive
earth change
spilling forth chaos
into the streets
of humanity

~ *We the people*
then
who want change
must learn
to speak up ~
in a more
effective manner
which goes
way ~ way beyond
what the people
do now
by just gathering
to occupy
some space
only to make
a little ruckus
not really giving
a noteworthy
statement
with a defined
direction
offering up
no more than
a mere presence
just marching

Nature ~ I Q : Let's Survive, Not Die !

or doing
that sit-in thing
grumbling on and on
while purpose
want and need
lay fallow ~
within
the underground
of obscurity

~ and don't get me wrong
I do believe in the right
of the people
to do such things ~

and yet people   ~

if we're gonna bring change
we gotta bring something
to the table
that's understandable
has sustenance
and has lasting value
for generations to come
other than saying   ~
we are some
Tea or Coffee Party
which at best
has a bland flavor
not distinct enough
to be remembered
or be used
by the people

offering nothing else
but a taste
with hardly an aroma
that's a diluted down
symbolism
from the past
inferring a revolution
yet no longer
as applicable
to the issues and needs
facing the people ~
today
nor too ~
the hopes and dreams
of the people
our children
our children's children
yet to come

We the people
need to communicate
to all ~
a clear cut message
'cause with
drastically disruptive
earth change
on the horizon
We the people
need to plan to adapt, transition
and transform
our lives
like the butterfly
to survive

Nature ~ I Q : Let's Survive, Not Die !

Photography by ~Keith Alan Hamilton~

a few more sayings ....

"We can assert our right to choose if we care to live on or not, whether we choose to do something or not to help assure humanity will live on into the future; and yet, despite if we choose not to live on, why would we not try to do our best to prevent a world that would rob our children and their children's children the same opportunity to have the right to choose; whether to be able to live on or not or to do something or not to help assure humanity will live on into the future?"

~ * ~

Nature ~ I Q : Let's Survive, Not Die !

Photography by Jenna Lindberg

~*~

"It seems prudent to question the logic shown by any people, who knowingly live on a dynamic planet that has a history of entire species coming to an end through environmental changes to impede the development of technologies; for instance a technology like space travel, which could be used to assure the survival of the people into the future."

~*~

Nature ~ I Q : Let's Survive, Not Die !

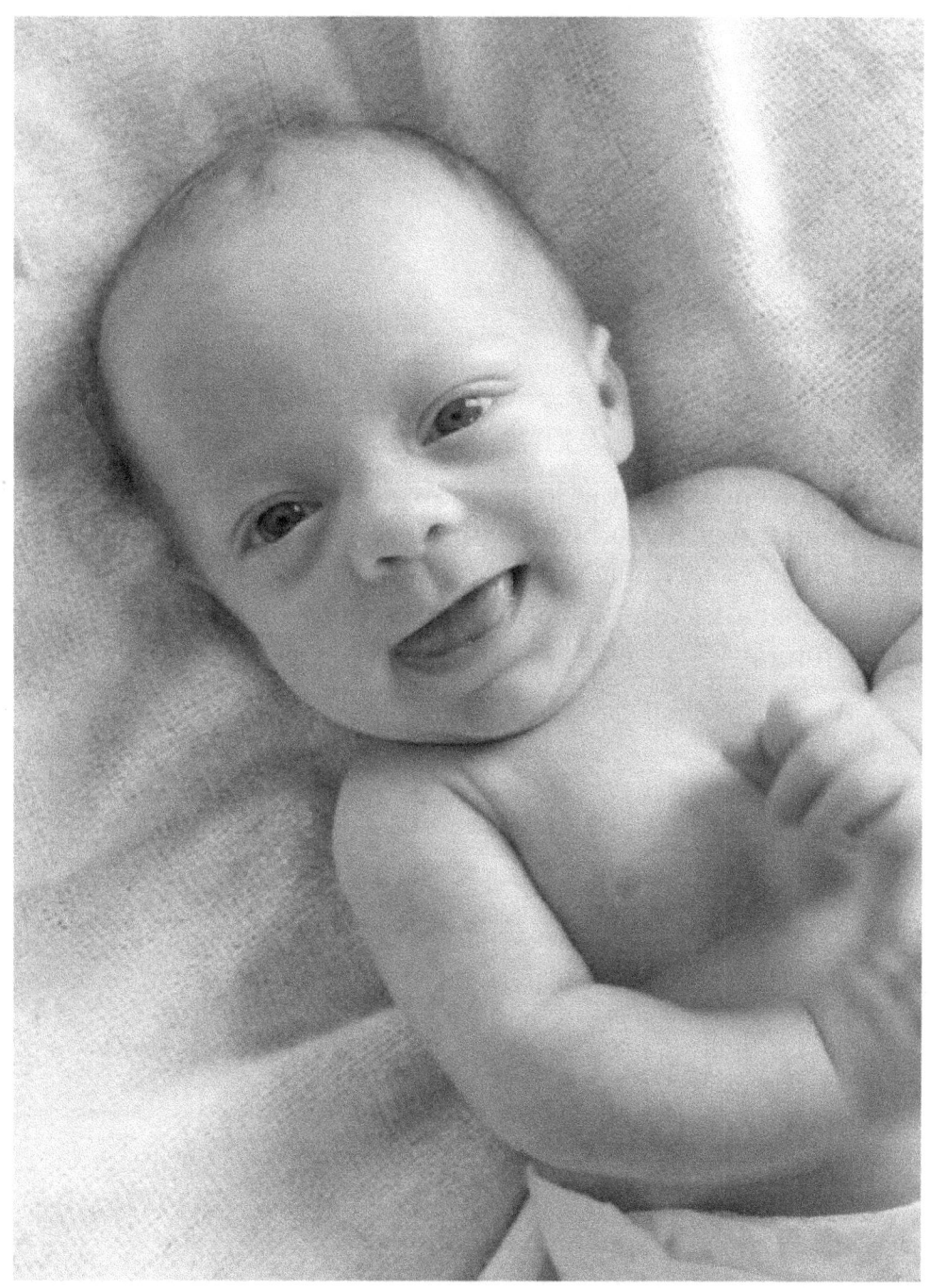

Photography by Jenna Lindberg

~*Keith Alan Hamilton*~

"People nagging others about lowering population growth, the carbon footprint or to plant trees and live sustainably, act as if they are intelligent enough to know how to fix the earth's destabilizing regulatory system solely through the process of mitigation; however, rather than nagging, maybe it's far wiser to use our time, while increasing our Nature ~ IQ to plan out how to survive earth destabilization through a process of proactive adaptation before such an occurrence has an effect on the demise of our species."

Nature ~ I Q : Let's Survive, Not Die !

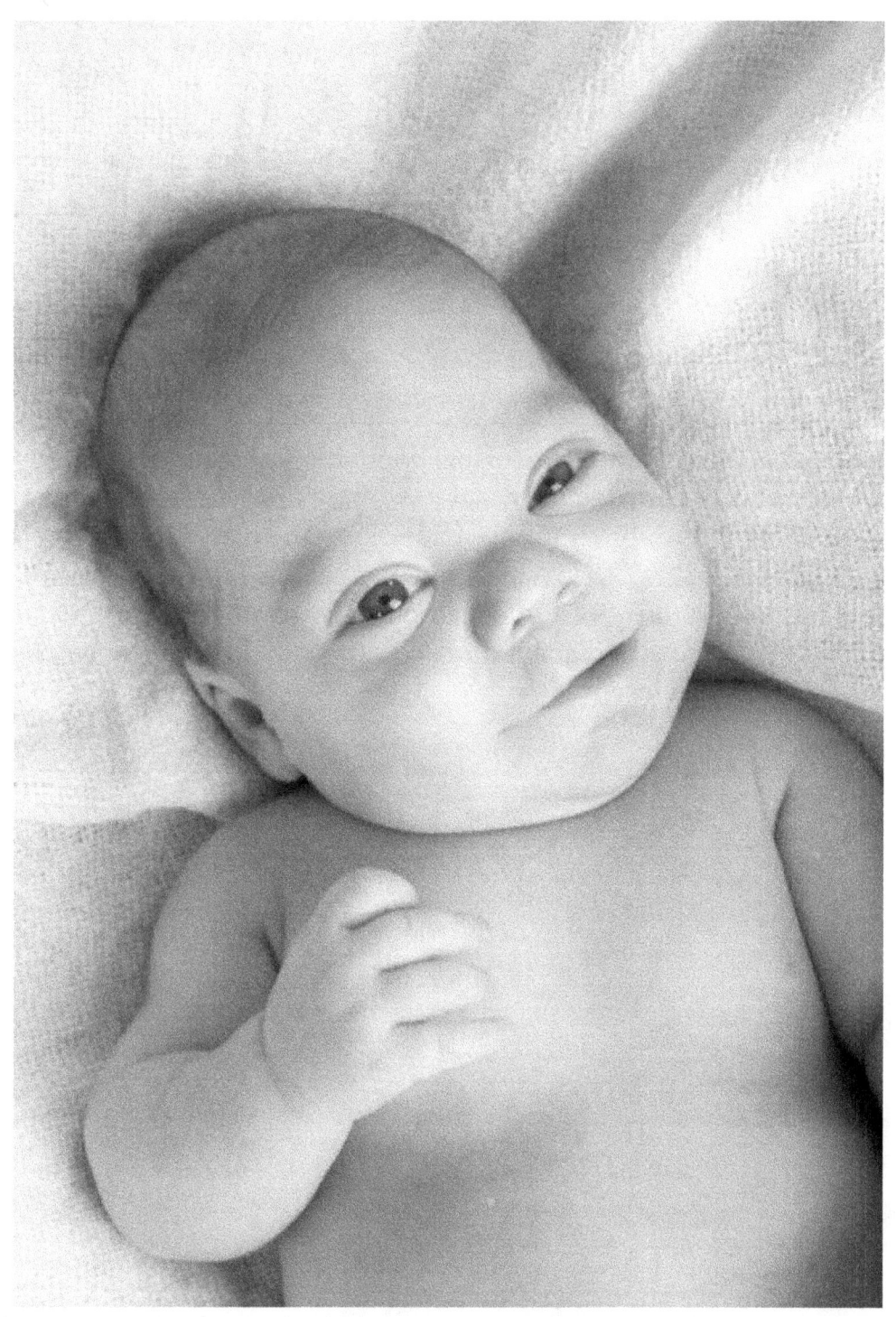

Photography by Jenna Lindberg

~ * ~

"It'll take great insight after much struggle through effort within the process of thinking together for humanity to sustain and then preserve its kind into the future; wherefore these would have to be intelligently perceptive insights, intelligently applied with our innovative technologies; thereafter implementing our insight and technology through primary and alternative contingency plans that will need to be flexible, preparatory, preventative and transitional in design; wherein scientifically being formulated around a more holistic understanding of the universal processes systemically regulating all of Nature as a whole system in the physical, not just the earth; as well as coming to the systemic realization that Nature's recurrent pattern of universal processes as they unfold and enfold through time are dynamic and not preordained or fixed; therefore certain aspects of Nature may need within the human process of intelligent progression to be modified through time to help sustain and then preserve humanity as a kind within time."

~ * ~

Nature ~ I Q : Let's Survive, Not Die !

~ * ~

"I'm sure, drastically disruptive earth changes to the human way of life, violent weather: hurricanes, tornadoes and extreme flooding on a global scale including plagues, nuclear war and terrorism, killer: super-volcanoes, asteroids, earthquakes, tsunamis or unfriendly extraterrestrials, etc., will inevitably occur, I say whatever: I'm confident as in the past, humanity will find happiness and purpose, emergent from the satisfaction found within the everyday struggle to survive; I'm also sure the future process of change upon earth will be an intelligently progressive lived experience to overcome, go on, if humanity prepares, plans ahead, even if through trial and error to find ways to proactively adapt to whatever obstacle Nature defiantly places before humankind."

~ * ~

~ * ~

"The time spent trying to intelligently progress the so-called human '*Larval Yokels'* in life within a process of knowing may be perceived just a waste of time or may be perceived overtime, well worth the struggle through effort; wherein, if deemed worthy, this struggle through effort may result in the continuance of all the systemic web of Nature as a whole system, being emergent upon the effect of a critical mass consciousness."

~ * ~

Nature ~ I Q : Let's Survive, Not Die !

Photography by Jenna Lindberg

~ * ~

"If given enough time we can do anything we want, if we continue to try, time may not be an adequate measure of intelligence because the struggle to know takes time and effort."

~ * ~

"If we together improve the overall wellbeing of the people, then unrest and violence will more than likely decrease among the people."

~ * ~

"If we together make information freely accessible to the people; where the people have the ability to become well-informed from experiencing a variety of perspectives; then the people will be less likely to be coerced into bringing harm to others."

~ * ~

~ * ~

"If we together are going to lead the people through word and deed, then we must also together layout a plan showing the people the way."

~ * ~

"To acquire the activist zeal and mindset for the 'cause' such as non-violence, to bring about change, the overall living condition of the people would need to be improved, changed, so the people could focus their attention on issues other than everyday sustenance."

~ * ~

Postface

Nature ~ I Q : Let's Survive Not Die !   ~Keith Alan Hamilton~

As mentioned previously, in 2012 I published this book without charge, online over the internet (flip-book and PDF formats), with the intent to increase the reach of its overall distribution. Now this print version has been added to the mix to help achieve the purpose of the book's various style of words.

When writing this book, contemplating how to publish it and then distribute it, I often thought of Thomas Paine. How valuable the printing press was in publishing his pamphlet Common Sense and then helping the information therein to become more freely accessible to others. What a timely and convenient blessing for those who were afforded the opportunity to weigh the most pressing issues, formulate opinions, and make decisions with a more diversified perspective.

It is within the same spirit that I've released my thoughts and words through poems, sayings and more, offering one more perspective to the overall mix so others, *We the people*, facing the most pressing issues of our day, like earth change, can formulate clear opinions and make well informed choices that lead to timely and sound decisions about humanity's future survival. How beneficial it would be if this process of cooperative and nonpartisan enlightenment could start now and could keep on transitioning beyond 2012 – the year that overflowed with doomsday prophecy and the rhetoric of politicians asking *We the people* to be elected without offering any concepts and practices that adequately deal with the issues of today and the most pressing issues of the future.

Maybe the concepts and practices herein will become the primer that will ignite *We the people* into being more proactive in shaping the outcome of our future. Maybe it will give *We the people* the basis to express our needs and wants more aptly and to formulate a united contingency of concepts and practices that can be offered to our much needed partners, those chosen by *We the people* to represent us within the government process. I pray and hope so.

~Keith Alan Hamilton~   Peace out!

Nature ~ I Q : Let's Survive Not Die ! ~Keith Alan Hamilton~

~Keith Alan Hamilton~

about the Author

~Keith Alan Hamilton~ is a poet/writer, Smartphone photographer and is the online publisher/editor of three blogs which includes the Keith Alan Hamilton.com Blog, the NatureIQ.com Blog and The Hamilton Gallery ~ Online.com Blog,.

Keith has been developing his spiritual philosophy, style of writing (poetry, prose, sayings, etc.) and photography for many years. The artistry of his words and photos are rooted within the nurturing arms of his Polish/German mother. Keith says his mother's willpower and loving temperament is the spirit flowing in his words and photos. They are also deeply influenced with the character of his Scot grandfather, who was a master storyteller and could hold his audience spellbound for hours on end. Keith's words and photos not only reveal the cultural flavor representative of his heritage but also the area in the USA where he was born. He grew up in a small place called Freeland, Michigan.

If Keith was asked to describe his style, he would say it embodies the everyday spirit of a Norman Rockwell illustration, a sort of raw Mark Twain individuality and the perfectionist mannerism captured in an Ansel Adams photo. Keith hopes his everyday style, that unique flavor tasted within the emergence of his words and photos, will appeal to a broad spectrum of people around the world..

~ * ~

Nature ~ I Q : Let's Survive Not Die ! ~Keith Alan Hamilton~

the Photographer ... Jenna Lindberg

I am a fine art wedding and lifestyle photographer.

*~ * ~*

I love beautiful things, quirky things and colorful things.

*~ * ~*

I am an observer.

Endorsements

I love the forcefulness of the words. All simply stated but with optimism, hope for the future and the proactive nature of we the people.

These pieces remind me of Whitman and Sandburg and Emerson whom I loved to read as a teenager.

Perhaps your words will entice our young people of today to go out and change the world and not complain about what has passed, not complain about what our government is not doing for us. Perhaps your words will entice we the people to take the lead and be responsible for our own world and our future in it.

Thank you Keith for your writing and wisdom. Thank you for sharing the beautiful photographs of your twin grandbabies. This is a wonderful and inspiring piece of work.

Madeline Sharples
Author of Leaving the Hall Light On

Nature ~ I Q : Let's Survive Not Die ! ~Keith Alan Hamilton~

The foundation of Keith's poems is "courage." Make that COURAGE, because Keith isn't worried about the usual work shopped-to-death poem one sees over and over again in magazines and on the internet. He wants his reader to see what he sees the way he sees it and that takes courage. He's risky. His line breaks come when he breathes. His verse is sometimes free, sometimes sculpted, sometimes danceable. His images walk straight into your mind and find their way to your heart with no detours, no missed turns.

I go to Keith's work when I want to feel real. When I want to know a "regulatory pattern/without hesitation/or remorse/on the earth's part."

A wonderful read! Thank you, Keith. Write on!

Martina Reisz Newberry
Palm Springs, CA 2012
Author of Learning by Rote

Nature ~ I Q : Let's Survive Not Die ! ~Keith Alan Hamilton~

Keith Alan Hamilton is a fabulously gifted Michigan poet, essayist and photographer. Nature ~ IQ is a beautifully written compilation of Keith's poetic works, filled with depth and insight into the world as it is and as it should become.

Denise Denomy
Photographer/Digital Artist

~ * ~

"Everyday free verse" says it all! In the tradition of Walt Whitman, Ez Pound and Gary Snyder arrives K A H.

With lines like "Fu k No", or "My mother has never...", or, "if we the people"- KAH gives refreshing American poetry! and good insights.
Highly recommended!

Dave Eberhardt
Poet/writer, Peace Activist and Mentor
Author of Poems from the Website, Poetry in Baltimore

Nature ~ I Q : Let's Survive Not Die !   *~Keith Alan Hamilton~*

Keith Alan Hamilton, crossed my path approximately 3 years ago. I am forever grateful for his presence in my life. He is one of the most sincere people that I know. He is unique, or as my Papa used to say – Uni-Q. He is a witty, sarcastic, loving, a fantabulous writer, supporter of the Arts and a highly intelligent human being.

Keith is as honest . . . as the aeons are long. If you do not expect to hear his opinion, don't ask. This sincere quality is a rarity in 'humanity', that I find refreshing, and appreciate so much. Keith, wears no mask !

I had the good fortune to meet him in person at a Poetry 'Gig' in Boston. Like a lot of us, he is a mixed bag of goodness and righteous anger. People talk about healing the world, and do nothing. This is not so with Keith. Keith is a DO-er. I have the utmost respect for the Man, Artist, Writer, Photographer and finally and certainly not least, my Eternal Friend.

Within the pages of Nature ~ IQ "Let's Survive, Not Die", you will see exactly what I mean. Buy one for yourself, and another as a gift. In doing so, you will be servicing humanity as well.

Janet P. Caldwell
Author

Nature ~ I Q : Let's Survive Not Die !   ~Keith Alan Hamilton~

First of all, Keith is an exceptional Human Being. For myself, this is where it all begins. He is a keen observer of the myriad of nuances that make up life. Being an observer he is quite adept at capturing aspects of the grand Human Involvement which is not always so comfortable to face for most of us. However, in doing so, confronting the sometime uncomfortable truths we are always the better for it. I applaud Keith, for courage to speak out is not one of his weaknesses.

Finally, when all the dust clears and we regain our vision as a collective, you will find Keith right there beside you, the rarity, is that he is an advocate for the evolution of goodness he purports throughout his work in Photography and Poetry and all that he chooses to involve himself with.

Blessings Keith

bill

William S. Peters, Sr.
Inner Child

~Keith Alan Hamilton~

Links

Websites

www.keithalanhamilton.com

www.natureiq.com

Flip Book

http://www.natureiq.com/intro/Default.html

Email

webmaster@keithalanhamilton.com

Inner Child Press

Inner Child Press is a Publishing Company Founded and Operated by Writers. Our personal publishing experiences provides us an intimate understanding of the sometimes daunting challenges Writers, New and Seasoned may face in the Business of Publishing and Marketing their Creative "Written Work".

For more Information

Inner Child Press

www.innerchildpress.com

intouch@innerchildpress.com